Paul Sutton
The Poetry of Gin and Tea
(A Satire)

KFS

Newton-le-Willows

Published in the United Kingdom in 2023
by The Knives Forks And Spoons Press,
51 Pipit Avenue,
Newton-le-Willows,
Merseyside,
WA12 9RG.

ISBN 978-1-912211-98-2

Acknowledgements:

Versions of some of these pieces first appeared in *International Times, Litter, Anthropocene, The Daily Sceptic*. Many thanks to their editors.

Contents

Contents

The Poetry of Gin and Tea
(A Satire)

PROLOGUE

All day I walked with a woman of lost memories
who knew everything I'd forgotten, 'just words',
she reassured. We stopped, looking back
down the canal at Bradford-on-Avon, lit
by a recurrent flicker, enough to wait for,
stood entranced by a long path of water.

Both pockets I'd once pat for reassurance are
now empty; but that long water again, how it
stretched and invited. Something had grown
unseen when not looked at, yet I can only
report not even a ripple to mar the lights
linking inner with outer existence. Who'd
question perception or if something was
there? I never thought to – just outside
then inside – as a lone figure,
could be walking away or not.

GIN

Its tincture captured by an industrial lightbulb.

A precious liquid perhaps, but easily spilt.

This Wiltshire hotel lounge was so empty, he could try three different armchairs finding the best light for his gin. Tilting the tenfold distilled Bathtub Imperial, he thought of Southwold, Norfolk, Hastings. Middle-class redoubts, where they sipped an imagined past, secretly craved but competitively attacked.

It was better than Victory Gin – and he was no Winston.

But Raven had been erased, which was almost a relief. Partly physical – his illness – his ego erupting, unworried at being exiled now his body already was.

So the elite enforced their selfish morality, constructed around confected identities – ripping out your ventricles if you refused to join them. At least in the past, when fealty was owed to some church, monarch, or government, just a few set the rules.

Now there were no 'barriers to entry', as they say about embarrassing inserts. Any twerp could get a degree, see suffering, then join the clergy without a church, grabbing razors to castrate those laughing at demands for evidence that life is inherited or women don't have testicles.

Could he use poetry to distil the abnegation, prostration – humiliation – he'd refused to display?

Paul Sutton

ABOLITION OF LITERATURE
(DREAMING OF ESTUARIES)

I.

Woke up with the word Shakespeare on his lips.

From outside came the echoes of crying.
People seeing their history in landfills:
forgotten presents, old Christmas annuals,

and our language – once free as open sea,
northern longships crossing freezing water –
is now bound, gagged, tortured in a cellar.

The simple joy of opening one's mouth,
swearing with the most 'offensive' words known:
'racist'; 'sexist'; 'homophobic' – just sounds.

The past not past, that's where I need to go.
I don't believe laughing at swinging tits
caused sex crimes or discrimination.

Nor did the execrable *Mind Your Language*
trigger anything but narcolepsy.
I say this, then a recent graduate

razor carves those words on my forehead.
'Bilbo woke up with the early sun in his eyes'.
Purity not ideology – cold air

cleaner than any thought now.
I can't believe they gave literature
away to haters, beckoned them in.

Who can bear their doctrines of perfection?
The sun over clouds, dreaming of escape –
absolute beauty of scientific truth.

II.

Landfill culture – psychogeographers –
there's nothing wrong with hating this country,
except you know hardly any of it.

We've been here before, obsession with the
Thames Estuary – Dickens, Conrad, Doyle,
doubtless too canonical, so instead

an exiled German in a terraced house,
missing – if honest – authoritarian
stamping, amazed by England's sloppiness.

Terrifying vistas over nothing –
sea-swill linking, somehow, to the Baltic –
but slapdash, give a fuck, English freedom.

No intellectuals, no dialectics,
no shining utopian futures – just
net curtains in a seaside greasy spoon.

So this wounded writer would imagine.
Daft really – childhoods still shone, like Christmas,
even better with North Sea waves slamming.

RAVEN ON GEMS

Outside, the January sunset gave a padparadscha display, flaming the sodden Wiltshire fields.

Sometimes he peered into his gemstones for hours. Raven was an obsessive collector from childhood. He felt they alone preserved any truth, refusing to deny reality for some semantic construct. This one on his finger, sparkling amethyst in candlelight, teal in sunlight; the science was unassailable. As was its beauty.

Raven had been stopped by an elderly Indian gentleman, shaking with excitement, asking its identity. The ring appeared bling, initially. Its exuberant Straits Chinese design combined muscularity with curved elegance. The startling alexandrite was 'dark horse': bitter lemon by day, purple into black at night. Over three carats and strikingly unincluded, other than from silk creating its inner glow.

He thought and talked such technicalities whenever he could. And the man had been interested, they'd even drunk coffee at Costa, on Hatton Garden. Raven haunted the area, remembering the Indian doing the same; a shop-owner, he claimed, always at his door or outside, aware if anyone slowed. He'd offered a card. Raven now found it shoved in his wallet and studied the photo of a star sapphire: rare Kashmir blue, with the delicate glowing celestial image at its centre.

The hotel grounds featured a few desultory fishing ponds, lone figures just visible under umbrellas.

Raven had fictionalised his nightmares.

THE LAKE

He wasn't sure if any heat came from the lake itself. Lazy bubbles of gas would surface when trudging its dull circumference. But everything here suggested heat, accumulated over millennia, exhaled onto his pale face.

He was exiled. The entire culture operated this way: fierce dialogue; joylessly febrile debate … then a roundup of anyone diverging from a pre-arranged consensus. The media trumpeted lists of the latest arrests. Progressives competed in hysterical outrage, damning those taken, demanding the most painful measures.

The treatments used extreme techniques. The combined academic, political, artistic worlds had decreed mankind needed returning to an equitable paradise. People could – by choosing 'ethnic realignment counselling' – accept. But refusal required enforced change, in the east African birthplace of humanity.

High above gaped ragged caves, sheltering man's earliest wall paintings. Progressives claimed such daubing foreshadowed figurative art, the discovery of perspective technique, even the 'invention of gravity' – since one showed a tree falling over.

And the truth? The scrawls were below the level of a three-year-old.

Raven blankly refused to visit. Queues of writers, artists, and academics, jostled in the heat to pay competitive homage, the desiccated lines stretching to the lake itself. Their enthusiasm would be closely monitored: a ten-minute presentation, then a lengthy tick-box document.

Solar noon, meridian sun.

He needed to get back soon, for his session.

These were extraordinarily painful. Every cell had to be swapped, requiring sixty drip infusions – via a PICC line – lasting five minutes each. Five hours, every fortnight.

Throughout, images flickered of his donor – an enormous LA drug dealer, celebrated as a saint by white liberals, after choking to death on a KFC when his mansion was raided.

The greater suffering was mental.

During the process, he was forced to recount anecdotes and long-buried memories from his childhood. These were to be made more 'diverse', converting his past into that of a youth raised in Tottenham, Peckham, or Harlesden.

For some reason, Raven could do so whilst remembering – yet concealing – his annual holidays with a distant uncle in the blue Shropshire hills.

Reciting the obvious poem to himself, various beepers signalled switches in the chemicals careering through his system. With practice, it could be timed so that the final line 'And cannot come again' coincided with each new toxin, the five minutes allowed him to slow every syllable, whilst robotically answering the nagging voices rewriting his life.

It was to be his only victory, but he never once divulged this land of lost content.

RAVEN'S PREFERRED READING

Written during chemotherapy, *The Lake*'s tone seemed distant and defeated. 'Racist' some claimed.

His favourite prose now? Unashamedly crime-based, antinomian, antisocial. He thought of a lesson last week.

'I'm reading the sort of book you used to say you loved and talked about all the time!'

A Passage to India; To the Lighthouse; Oranges Are Not the Only Fruit; The Collected Poems of Carol Ann Duffy?

What lunatic would enthuse about such stodge to Year 8 students?

The girl shyly flashed its title: *Interviews with Serial Killers, Part 1 – Ted Bundy, The Unabomber and Jeffrey Dahmer.*

He'd pay thousands to hear her usual teacher.

'FANTASTIC you have a book. But what are you reading?'

'Oh, Mr. Raven recommended it'.

'Wonderful! Let's have a look at the cover ... '

Paul Sutton

NO STOPS FOR MURDER

Culture war, so the day pubs reopened
mostly the middle classes stayed away.

I saw one in the Co-op, still masked –
almost a surgical gown – he looked half-angry
when asked, was he going to 'Independence Day'.

Well, there I was, my book on Ted Bundy to read –
the anonymity of gas stops, stolen credit cards and
Holiday Inns. A man in a zebra tie said he believed
in reincarnation – after five pints – and thought this
life was pathetic. He'd go out as dust to planets
and beyond. His dour friend said this life was enough,
a miracle, if you took time to sort fine from the rough:
who wants to come back as atoms in another place?

Planes were invisible above the clouds,
not spying, but not free to wander wide
over the earth's curve, out to the zone
where blue meets gold.

RAVEN'S CRIMES

Where did his love of crime-writing originate? Violence, experienced in his early school years at a rough outer, outer, outer London comprehensive? That dread of 'being beaten up' hanging in the air, the incredible fights witnessed and run from.

He'd taken refuge in the Sherlock Holmes stories, which he reread with increasing frequency, never travelling far without his battered Collected. These he rewrote as lovingly revolting pastiches, misunderstood as merely humorous. They only worked in an Appendix ...

In truth, he'd never committed any crimes but speeding, drunk driving – and firing an air-rifle from a high-rise Bristol flat at a line of noisy irritants queuing for a trans-nightclub. He'd aimed at and hit the swinging sign above their heads.

Perhaps this counted as a hate crime. He'd certainly been filled with it when he pulled the trigger. Firing down into modernity from a converted office building.

Paul Sutton

BEYOND BOREDOM INTO BEDFORDSHIRE

The start was concrete
with water into heat – no
shelter from it – scurrying
backwards to my yeasty flat.

Made it.

I can now list all those
temporary particulates –
this does me no good.

But first, imagine a man
paid to sit in a box on a
bridge, taking five pence
from every motorist.

As a job, it has limits.
Possibilities are endless.
Some would stay aloof,
pretending indifference.

Geoffrey Plovdiv, who coughed
over HR's footsteps, taken for
some kindness training. He
had every worthless degree
known to humanity, fell through floor
after floor, landed in base analytics and
found himself in a childhood without his
children – no sound, just absence.

The bridge's owners think strategy –
investment and potential for growth.

Poor Geoff. Mostly people paid, but
some would drop gum or After Eight
Mints into his hairy paw. I winced
as he begged for tenure at the
University of Central Bedfordshire,
the job taken by a serial killer
turned criminology professor.

Paul Sutton

THE GOLDEN AGE

O to write a story, but plot foils me.

A huge estate, centring on parkland,
in the middle a Victorian house and
a recluse who knows every detective
story from The Golden Age. Yet now,
writing, I drip anonymity, airport retail.

I need to sublimate, produce literature.

And that recluse? He reads in our estate pub,
the solitary gent – not cyclist, thank God –
ill-suited to a menu of forced jocularity but
how I admired his ability to stand in a road,
avoiding all the traffic. Apparently, his house
once loomed sentinel in the middle of a field –
then came the bypass – and last the estate.

Legend has it, he shot various working class
youths who besieged his abode, though
a compromise was found when he emerged
as an aging English teacher, at the local comp.

Lord, how he tore up that culture, to ram
the shreds down gaping throats. A serial
killer within a year, then moorhen shooter,
now a licensed slave trader supplying
progressive businesses lumpen fodder
for every cause – from boiling oceans to
the taxonomy of genitalia in public toilets.

Prodigious, the output from his drinking!
Like 'Basil', from the Hatton Garden heist,
our man was generosity itself in Wetherspoons.
Breakfasts were bought for all – especially he
adored the Ming dynasty blue-China plates,
the bottomless coffee cups. The violence
when the machines jammed was incredible.

Paul Sutton

OF HOLIDAYS I'VE TAKEN – THE ODDEST

So many true crimes I'd stalked,
declaring serial killers – their fables
available in garden centres – wolves
of today, tearing at the flabby ankles
of fractured society, dragging victims away
to flickering afterlives on reconstructions seen
in bedsits, ag-lab council houses, garish estates.
The only popular artform left to us!

I planned a tour of sacred locations
only to find one readily available,
with Premier Inn accommodation,
video shows, quizzes, fancy dress;
Fred Dinenage (official biographer
to the Krays) was the guide.
Clydach came first.
What to wear?

A deer-stalker plus cape
might seem incongruous.
How about leisure gear from that
retail park by the M4 Bridgend exit?
Dawn saw me heading over the Bridge,
breakfasting in the lower Swansea valley.
An early stop for some suitable clobber,
then the bliss of newbuilds

framed against steep valleys.
I saw Fred's auburn sideburns
plus combover at 8.29am,
a minute early for registration,
earnestly in conversation with
the newly retired hangman
of Singapore. A large chap
in crumpled pinstripe suit.

'My icebreaker is to estimate
drops for everyone in the bar,
LADIES FIRST!' he chortled,
grabbing Fred in a neck-lock.

Paul Sutton

RAVEN'S HATRED

He felt it now. The effect of relentless censorship and 'be kind' propaganda, policed by people bubbling with loathing. After a lunchtime discussion with colleagues, Raven was charged with biological determinism, for saying that the England men's football team would soundly beat the women's. His claim was 'not evidence based' – even if the men did win, 'it didn't mean they were any better at football'.

Raven pleaded guilty. He believed men and women were defined biologically. Dislike for this scientific truth made no difference to its veracity. And if they said winning in sport didn't mean you were better, they knowingly asserted nonsense. Most terrifying was their nervous zeal, competing to attack; as if the stronger their denials of reality, the more progressive they all were. One assured him: 'I don't *think* you're sexist – I shan't be cancelling you'.

Giving thanks for this wonderful news, he asked how it fitted with their claim 'cancel culture doesn't exist'.

A week in Coventry ensued, then he was invited to a 'friendly but informal meeting' and threatened with disciplinary action.

DISTILLATION

No doubting it, most colleagues wanted him dead.
An odd feeling, familiar to anyone disagreeing with woke beliefs.
Teachers are masters at scowling tuts; easy to know you're in disgrace.
They weren't worried about plotting his execution, in the corridor.
Their strength was the swiftness in denunciation then damnation.

Distillation of hatred gives a universal gas, in classes, stairs, offices.
A majority there are progressives: anxious; overwhelming; deadly.
A sacrifice is needed, an offering to their insatiable religion,
for fear its gaze could fall on them. He sat fixed to his chair –
they came for him anyway.

RAVEN'S MISSION

The problem now was how to use this febrile energy. Words were not enough. What appealed was the idea of breaking and entry: leaving turds on granite work tops; ineradicable skids on floral throws; stretched cocks and balls, scrawled on a Grenfell Tower poetry anthology *Phoenix from the Flames*.

Revoltingly better than the tightest piece of writing; or was the gin thinking for him, fantasising Bolano-type visceral realism?

Logic and reasoning were now dismissed as expressions of power, so he'd assert his own. Not as some Raskolnikov. His intentions were selfish and humorous – only he need find them funny.

Perhaps he'd done this through teaching, but indirectly, at considerable personal cost and never directed at pupils. Now was the time to silence ambiguity. Counselling hadn't worked either.

CBT

How's sex?

Well, into one's fifties …

Try dogging. Lay-bys and fading dinner ladies –
the headlights hide everything.
I have a list of postcodes.

Sorry, no satnav.

What about aggro?
A dig in the ribs, clipping of heels at the school-gates –
parents flying – progressives yell 'micro-aggression'.

Jostling at the cash-machine;
excavation of their back lawn;
excrement through the letterbox.

Or a nightclub punch-up.
The aesthetics of aftershave – a grab for some tits;
bouncers launching to separate you and boyfriend.

You're supposed to be my counsellor.

It's therapeutic, efficacious for both:
Ritualised. We all hate each other
since the Brexit vote.

Like strutting Indian/Pakistani border guards?

Racist simile.

RAVEN'S TARGET

In divine reification, a man entered the gin lounge.

Ironic smile, ironic *everything*, even at a cellular level. Human, perhaps, but those restraints went when such jerks reversed the Enlightenment. They can't enter a room without making everyone's shit itch – cringing, unsettling, sneering – expecting gratitude for their presence. A meaningless qualification from a motorway service station, convincing them their views are rigorously 'evidence-based'.

The jerk studied the gin menu, with occasional guffaws. He recited some of the fifty varieties in an affected drawl, like a mockney version of Kenneth Willliams impersonating Will Self.

Raven eyed him. What sort of violence would he want inflicted on this irritant? Tom Ripley amused himself with such questions. Recent 'social justice' rioting and destruction, frequent deaths, made objection meaningless. The highest legal authorities in England and the United States were unequivocal: if an individual felt some injustice oppressing them, they were entitled – obliged – to use physical force.

How could progressives object? They approved their own violence: blocked roads; smashed statues; the destruction of people and businesses. Of course, hypocrisy would define their rebuttals. Jackboots into genitals.

Societies without free expression, legitimised by claims of fighting oppression, ended this way. Whatever they might claim, he was of the old British Left. Its non-ideological heroes, especially Orwell, had championed freedoms of belief, thought and speech. Raven detested the progressives' nebulous mantras, disguising their terror for fair debate and love of censorship, returning us to a medieval hierarchical society – ritualistic – with them the pitiless controllers.

Children were once spared, but soon enough now, Caliban replaces Ariel, dogmatism freedom of spirit, flatulence perfume ...

Strange, when you can no longer rely on your own body. Radical surgery made his digestion (at best) dubious, often explosive. With just one other person present – clearly an idiot – he felt no embarrassment. His concern was to ensure the effect was utterly undisguised, incapable of being taken for a chair-scraping or car revving. The sound of a sail ripping, or a Hercules transport plane from Brize Norton, circling Seacourt Tower? He struck just as the Jerk lispingly announced:

'Blind Tiger – a refined Belgian gin, fragrant & delicate with a nod to woody juniper. A touch of bitterness'.

The coward feigned deafness. He momentarily flicked his eyes across at Raven; a social examination, to check if he knew his assailant. Satisfied, he went back to a faked reading of the gin menu.

'Having difficulty deciding?' Raven asked.

A yellowy grimace – half admonishing, half-pleading – the only response. But he could see that a mobile phone was being tapped; pictures of Raven had been slyly snapped; immediate pings made it obvious.

'Don't be shy – you can record my next one; it's brewing nicely!' Raven mocked. 'Maybe a selfie – if you fancy the aroma in this corner?'

The Jerk rose and stormed to the bar. Raven overheard a muffled conversation, someone called Emily tittering obediently as the incident was retold. The Jerk allowed himself to be easily dissuaded from 'having it out with that arsehole!'

In the corner of the lounge sat a pile of old board games. Hipsters manufactured nostalgia for these, though none were old enough to have played them in childhood.

Raven was.

INVENTION OF BOARD GAMES

You remember – incredibly complex
rules – maybe your father would read
then pronounce, expert, who moved first,
how you retrieved gemstones (Buccaneer),
when to guess villain, room, weapon?

The most baffling was Colditz, no wonder
hardly anyone escaped. I think stealing the
Commandant's car was the only possibility,
or making a glider out of German underpants
and Red Cross parcels containing balsawood.

Well, I invented one, though it mainly needs
telepathy. You write a word on a single sheet,
then somehow the person to your sunrise side
guesses away. I'm worried it sounds like a
writing game, played on poetry courses.

RAVEN'S HISTORY

Perhaps Raven's confrontational nature was epigenetic and instinctive. All those battles triggered by what felt like existential threats. Not far buried in his family's past were chronicles of genocide and exile. The last was romanticised now, by those who'd left hellholes for shelter in this country. Feelings of anger, guilt – perhaps inadequacy – created irrational loathing for England and the English. He understood, yet despised this response, explored so tediously in Contemporary Literature.

No good deed goes unpunished, as the French remind us.

How he loved snooping in hotels. A sudden snowstorm, distracting the few staff, allowed him to sneak into their private quarters, housing – of course – eastern Europeans. Most were wildly overqualified for a role buttering up progressives fleeing from themselves.

One lady had a doctorate in Slavic Literature, thesis propped on the mantelpiece in her squalid attic room. He leafed through it. Patricia Dubrowaska had spent years exploring the existence of pan-Slavic identity, never imagining its manifestation in lonely hospitality workers throughout England. By her bedside stood a photograph of two blond girls and a brooding man, in what looked like Cracow.

We all know Orwell's description of a hopeless slum girl unblocking a drain near Wigan. Raven popped down to his room and picked up his *Collected Prose* – without which, as with the Holmes anthology, he never travelled.

The Road to Wigan Pier exhaustively chronicles domestic poverty, at its worst in bedrooms. His mother had slept on packing cases as the child of penniless Greek refugees. After deliberating, he tore out the page and left it on the woman's pillow.

If this made any sense, he'd no idea. It felt right to him but would probably seem insane to most.

Who knew with anything now?

Only poetry captured his maternal family's story.

He hesitated for longer, then left her the poem.

Paul Sutton

DREAMING FOR THE ENGLISH

Sleep is an avalanche I'm hoping for,
to powder over the past and present –
leaving only a child's whiteness that
waits with patience for a single step.

I'm haunted by how they found him –
George Mallory – clasping the mountain.
One dead English, toughened old leather,
bound like a hoop. I'm proud of those two,
last seen through a gap in the clouds
crawling to the summit, falling through
all time and standing grinning in tweeds.
No sign of fear or doubt or the crimes
fools think our country was written by.

We have been ill – are ill – yet remain well.
This is our place, one made by boredom
or madness – glory all around – in gaps
between smashed gates and roadworks.

I'm researching my lost Greek grandfather.
The horrible old sod who swam somehow
from Smyrna to Athens, then London. His
city was burned by the Turks – birthplace
of Homer and Europe – whipped to the sea.
Horses' legs smashed, the boats capsized –
bodies floating as jetsam. He was a bastard
who beat my yiaya and abused my mother.
Violence is a solid you can't swallow which

sticks in your throat and needs spitting out.
Now dawn. How I love this grey of English
watercolour, tracing a gorgeous suburb
where stories somehow start or end.

RAVEN'S LOVE OF SUBURBIA

What supposed liberal doesn't laugh at suburbs, modern estates, retail parks, theme parks, New Towns and Garden Cities?

But those *are* this country. Not the absurd areas of regeneration carved out from stomping grounds for serial killers, 60s gangsters and 90s psychogeographers. Nor the ossified rural areas; he sat in one now – aching in its beauty – swamped with four-by-four lunatics.

In truth, it's difficult to work out where left-liberals DO want to live. As with everything, their tutting dissatisfaction, and an absence of identity other than 'arsehole', makes this question vexed. In theory, they like edgy areas in large cities, but only when these are safely gentrified and the working classes priced out, banished to easily avoidable estates and – above all – to schools their offspring attend.

Raven was born in central London. He'd been moved, very early, out to Welwyn Garden City. A place so lacking in history, it was perfect for his simple memories of warmth, childhood – happiness.

WELWYN GARDEN CITY

I.

I cannot think of anywhere less apt
to set – say – a ghost story or fable
of regeneration. But it haunts me
now, the boulevards billowing absurd
cherry blossom, or the constant poplars,
gardens then allotments, and lone horses
in fields nobody owned (though somebody
did). We don't know if everywhere from
childhood does this; I only have the one.

Imagine if Wordsworth had grown up here.
Some daft sister, avowed book devourer,
who chronicled his conkers and fainted –
her stolen bike; his lost virginity!
It's useless. The place was an escape zone
from Orwell's 'rotting nineteenth-century
houses' – my grandparents', in Shepherd's Hill,
with rickety stairs and views to Archway.

Teachers' faces, quiet optimism.
I grew up to fight with idealism,
middle class deceit over origins.
None of which matters now, at all, to me.

I also don't know if the violence
which meandered, natural as the Mimram,
was some thawing relic, or new death pains
from our vanishing culture of content.

II.

On how many home-county Sundays
did my father drive us to some stately pile,
plonked on emerald parkland, tramping
endless overheated rooms?

Let's face it, this was the 1970s,
before suburban housing filled
with numerous foreigners. I've long
kept secret – Winston Smith like –
my shameful nicknames for them.

Cut to hatchet-faced anger.

My grandparents were
mothball-reeking Greeks –
wops or greaseballs. They
lived in Highgate, then
Muswell Hill: terrifying
Victorian housing;
enclosing leaf mulch
concealing serial killers.

Our estate was unique:
everyone was an idiot.
Some fools opening
their houses to visitors,
claiming 'dinner parties'.

Even now, our rentier class –
shipwrecked, washed up –
continues this brutal charade.

Who can eat in someone
else's house? Insane to
ask, but I'm a veteran of
cheek-clenching fiascos.

I now never do so.

And who cares where we
all live. It's enough to bask
and brew strong tea, wait
for the future to do what
it's always wanted to do.

TEA

A sacred drink, bringing back his father. The only person allowed to make it in Raven's childhood home.

Dad got up before everyone else. They'd awaken to his morning brew, always leaf tea. Raven had been amazed to discover, from old cardboard boxes at school, that some families used tea bags or ate shredded wheat.

Welwyn Garden City was the epicentre for this revolting cereal, with its resemblance to rats' nests or aged pubic hair. Nabisco silos loomed over the poorest parts of the town, by the 1920s railway station and mildewing older estates.

How terrible that it wasn't safe to order tea, even in a hotel like this. One got a muslin pouch of potpourri, producing something tasting of pencil shavings.

Raven was reading the Raffles stories. They were stunningly subversive, so well-crafted as to shame modern writers. Their elegant insouciance – triumph, disgrace and death, mixed with high-jinx capers – intoxicating. Less highly flavoured than the Holmes stories, yet harder to imitate.

Orwell had known how to make real tea! And then *Raffles and Miss Blandish* compared Raffles' innocent crimes with 'modern' savagery. God knows what he'd say now, about Raven's insane criminal longings. Presumably he'd be busier with the more important issue: a vertiginous collapse in freedom of speech and thought. Not through repressive governments, but from the self-destructive sabotage of 'liberals'.

Raven simply had to attack. His hero eviscerated the linguistics of modern tyranny but not the ceaseless moralising of those whom C.S. Lewis warned 'torment us for our own good, without end, for the approval of their own consciences'.

Raven fought such people daily – and lost. He'd been doing so since 1982 and could enumerate (probably elucidate) fifteen-thousand confrontations. In most, he'd been too cowardly or concerned and had hopelessly acquiesced in his own defeat.

It was only since his illness that he'd decided on free-speech absolutism as the only sane act.

It would also fail, but at least he wouldn't be on the winning side.

His writing was the way now – if he could only be honest. When he looked back over this trivial evening in a gin bar, it would be absurd to pretend, even to himself, that he could use it for anything but a laconic TripAdvisor review.

His safest memories from childhood? Those baths when the water was so hot it seemed impossible, lowering in an almost unendurable agony. But then you were under – you sometimes even shivered. Your private parts would shrivel up, as they now did in the Thames when he free-swam from spring to autumn.

What a fix! From such hot-water days he'd stretched out – alone – to find an entire industry and economy, a culture, hierarchical and clambering, its apex constant awards for struggles with identity and ethnicity.

But the texts! Never had mankind been so blessed. Production was uncontrolled, except by mentors and experts, throwing rope-ladders down to mendicants, supplicants thrashing through the icy waters.

He'd got one foot out, one spidery hand onto a rung. Someone in London grabbed his thinning thatch – he was saved – but ideology unsound sucked him down, beneath the dying swimmers, into the depths where madmen fought over pillaged wreckage.

Identical yet bigger and better, the firework displays far above, the lectureships and Masonic networks, tentacles twitching through our lassoed culture, strangling dissenting voices.

Raven had taught *London* too many times not to know the harlot's curse, not to smash his brains out on those palace walls.

You bastards, hypocrites, witches – your treasures are toilet paper for odourless faeces.

TOWNS OF LOST DOGS

How they bark at night
sometimes on dark estates
other times running by rails
far into empty lands as
dreams wait like friends
you left before you
saw them grow just
fractions of our lives in
a new town with vast
boulevards from those
first autumn schooldays
where long years fall
and a late sun fools
us things last.

SUCH, SUCH WERE THE JOYS

When did he first hear today's mantra: 'Am I allowed to say this … ?' Hadn't the instinctive rebuttal once been: 'It's a free country, isn't it?'

Any true writer adores language's pure power, knows how it works distanced from action. They're linked, but current censorship insisted there was no distinction.

A teaching discussion, on *The Sign of Four*; no interest in it as literature, simply condemning it as 'racist' and 'sexist'.

'I don't care', he'd snapped.

Raven extolled its plot, characterisation, prose – the ambiguity in Jonathan Small's relationships with the Indian characters. He'd met blank stares then impatient interruption.

When did such self-censorship capture our minds and tongues?

What word would Raven write, in his invented board game?

He grabbed a gin menu and – without embarrassment – wrote the surname, then the full real name as it appeared on his grave, in Sutton Courtenay by the river Thames. The village was ten miles south of Raven's home, one of many Suttons he knew.

Orwell understood you needed to reclaim your childhood – fresh and inviolable – before some ideologue tore it up. Raven worried it was too late for his own – both parents gone – only his obsessions to focus on.

John Cowper Powys showed how, in *Weymouth Sands*: ' … seizing upon some dominant or poetical aspect of the physical present … a fresh, a simple, a childish enchantment – the mystery of life reduced to the most primitive terms … as long as he could feel the presence of these things *in a certain way* – as a child goes to sleep clutching tightly some fragment of wood or cardboard or twisted tin … '

CROSSING THE ALPS

I.

On a plane, over dizzying white purity,
a seven-year old's first package holiday.

Glimpsing impossible peaks then
minuscule villages with monstrous
cataracts from heart-ache glaciers.

Jesus! Off to Tunisia, how the 1970s
opened up, from flat orange browns
to cobalt blues and towel-gowns.

I got burned in Hammamet, awoke
convinced a Tsunami was breaking.

No worries. Dad bought me Roman coins
in Carthage. He smuggled them through
Tunis customs hidden in his old socks –
as if they gave a toss.

Luton Airport – that was the Mecca
for travel – with colours which hurt
and queues to the carpark. In truth

the architecture was such a glory,
ugly for sure but just optimism,
not spoilt-brat irony.

II.

All the towns I've
walked around
often in the autumn
tracing steps back to some
cathedral or shopping centre
but mostly standing in the rain.
That cold clean force whatever one
wore it would soak through into me
now and forever. Plates would be
moving under a distant ocean –
tearing worlds apart – all I had was
some lonely shop still lit on a late
Saturday afternoon – a panicked
purchase, though glorious, an album
or an army surplus jacket. Last bus
back over the sodden Salisbury Plain
incredible the blasting of autumnal rain
careering through rickety villages strung
along empty A-roads, not the steppe
or the Chinese belt-and-road initiative
taking our flag for takeaway. But then
who's not happy in some pearl-glinting
paradise suffused with the east; do you
know how long they sailed to ride the
monsoon winds from the Cape to the
Indian coast then Cathay? Goods yet
unknown, t-shirts and cheap shoes
but I'm not sneering, it's communal to
shop and beautiful. Better than rotting
on Edwardian literature which I love to
do. A ghost story about a man hanged
because the priest wouldn't betray a
confessional. Well, faith has its place
but I prefer just the rain again.

HOW DID THE HIGH MOUNTAINS VANISH?

He sat slumped. The gin had done what it always did, but at least he wasn't in The Chestnut Tree café, a waiter dripping syrup in his drink.

Winston had searched for the past in some London 'prole' pub.

Could Raven even remember people not looking scared when speaking?

Because literature needed people who thought and spoke freely. He recalled a piece about a shared sleeping compartment on a stifling Indian train. Too hot to sleep, Orwell and an unknown travelling companion drank whisky all night, damning the British Empire, revelling in their freedom of speech then parting at dawn like guilty lovers. He discusses the corrosive effect of selling yourself in public, buying yourself back in private. But at least the language used for both was then free.

The problem now was deranged idealogues, ignorant of Enlightenment values.

Within every revolutionary lurks a hangman.

English is the language of free enquiry, the plain-spoken enemy of hypocrisy and tyranny: gloriously vulgar; precise; energetic; abusive. But once these haters controlled it, that inheritance was doomed.

Perhaps their hatred was because no ideology had ever used it as a mother tongue. He could hear them sneering: 'Duh! What about capitalism?' But that was human nature, its wonders, imperfections, horrors.

The education system was bloated with such charlatans, wrecking our language through envy, shame, and self-loathing. They patrolled their ugly flatlands with fanatical ruthlessness, devoid of pity and humour, persecuting any flickers of individuality – human nature itself.

But those peaks still tower above their featureless plains – somewhere.

Paul Sutton

NOW IS SCHOOL SUMMER

It's the greens, the infinite shades
dragging me to 1978 playing fields.
The heat at midday seems tropical,
the girls sway off to smoke under
poplar trees, as 'Miss You' plays.

Indoors, even more memories.
The bottled light, devastating,
the toilets for fighting.
Now joy from images,
torpor, the smell from

pavements, the risky cut-throughs
overgrown, with lurking 'yobs' still
wearing flares – skateboarding as
freedom risking a kerb. Who cares
but me. If that's enough I don't know.

It needs writing then tightening.
Almost exhausted before the urge
slackens, my grip loosens. Words
are forced into place but won't stick.
Something was there and isn't now.

A fifth verse for each of five lines.
Symmetry, but will anyone notice.
If I trudge uphill back to my old
school, I'll arrive then have to leave.
I could get in my car and go there now.

ONLY PITY MATTERS

How I feel it when I see some lone child
walking slowly to school, that fearful look
as they get near, eyes flicking either side,
ears alert for any nickname, hoping
to get inside unseen, to find shelter
unremarked, ignored. Even worse is the
pretend happiness when all feels empty.

Pity is something that can't be taught, which
comes from walking home without any friends,
never being asked, from hearing others
laughing at your pain. My colleagues over
some old fool dismissed – 'inappropriate
comments' – forfeiting his job, pension, life.
Luckily, they 'felt sorry for the wife'.

Paul Sutton

CODA

In the mountains
nothing changes.
Air unbreathed
for centuries, the
sharp peaks, clouds,
blue skies. Footprints
are nothing, only snow
and ice mean a thing.
One night, landscapes
change – landlocked
countries open to
the sea. An age of
people you knew,
they now speak.

IN FRONT OF YOUR NOSE

Raven saw it all now.

Sat transformed through radical surgery and treatment; by selfless people to whom he owed his life.

One he'd spent running from the middle classes:

Box-set evenings; dinner parties; 'expert' worshippers; monolithic diversities; invented complexities; converted Victorian houses; competitive anxieties; eating disorders; unlimited gender pronouns; class hatreds; mockneys; failed promotions; meaningless qualifications; nihilistic affairs; gender realignments; elbowing park runs; gym memberships; cyclists blocking rural roads; lap-top jockeys; artisanal coffee shops; homicidal friendships; downsizing consultants; lactose-intolerants; disgraced frottagers; gap-year kidnappers; coastal town regenerators; sock-sniffers; beard-cultivators; ethnicity inventors; instant epidemiologists; fridge enviers; Anglophobics; Brexit-haters; mask wearers, Waitrose cosmopolitans; deputy-heads' wives dogging with Moldovan builders; evidence-based practitioners who 'know the science'.

Running to what?

Paul Sutton

HOLD ONTO ME FOREVER DAD YOU SAID

Let me hear it in my dreams till I die.
Water of blue champagne, Sardinian sky,
you staring down at fathomless teal shade,

nothing to fear, certain that it won't fade,
sure you could keep all you ever needed
in your grasp – 'jump together', you pleaded –

clasping hands plunging into Neptune's Cave.
If pictures are to keep, it's this I'll save.
And you standing alone on Ventnor sand,

your arms reaching out, another island.
What I'll not see, years from now,
is snow falling on streets through

soft city lights – and you staring up
laughing with just music and a boy.
Not worrying. Everything for the

moment, no past nor future.
Dawn on another landscape,
on days which vanish west.

* * *

I see you speeding past dark doors heading for one,
light at the end of a drive. Some houses scare you
and others aren't noticed. Who knows when it is,
but I won't be anywhere or maybe only in words if
this is kept somewhere, somehow, even after
our invasion and dilution which happened so

at least must be told. It's not an insult to notice,
just as I'd tell my father which of these houses
we'd passed I'd hate to live in, now you do the same,
not knowing how immense what you say is and
how even the basic plot for a life is beyond any
comprehension. This village we drive to for your

after-school maths, not a streetlight even though
larger than our suburb. I hope I'll keep everything
you've said, the freeness in your never having heard
of Pelé or Moore; does it matter what people know?
I'm tired of sharing what I do – usually very little –
as this narrow lane shows us some deer running

madly through our headlights unable or unwilling
to jump. Or a creeping of things – I use the words
too aware – so that darkness, when it's here,
seems to have been coming and we knew it,
but just like a thing in some or other book,
maybe sadness. Let's enjoy surfaces.

Paul Sutton

EPILOGUE

What is a life but those you leave behind –
with they and theirs then leaving others too?
'so much', I said, 'so much', and then I left.
Just said goodbye, but when I shut the door,
you stayed still here, tucked tightly all alone.
The days which last can never be our own.

(For Helen Sutton, nee Economides, 12th January 1933 – 3rd February 2022)

APPENDIX

THE SQUATTING THOMAS AFFAIR

I returned to Baker Street for several weeks, during that bleak winter of 1895. My beloved wife's Aunt Agatha was breathing her last, after an interminable struggle with dropsy, phlegmatic fever and vaporising delusions. As an experienced medical practitioner, I had long despaired of any improvement, but Mary felt obliged to decamp for the wilds of Bridport, where the nonagenarian glowered in grim isolation on the Dorset coast.

Holmes was himself then at a low ebb, much frequenting the meanest opium dens of Limehouse and Shad Thames. As I stared gloomily out at the London miasma of traffic, yellow smoke and huddling humanity, my friend moved for the first time in several hours, passing me a stained and tattered manuscript.

'Brother Mycroft has sent me this account of disturbing events, in Weymouth, written by a semi-literate graduate of Durham University – one Cornelius Griswald – now reduced to tutoring pallid adenoidal youths.'

I immediately devoured this extraordinary document, punctuated as it was with curry sauce blotches and tiny fragments of fried fish batter:

The Legend of Squatting Thomas, as recorded by Cornelius Griswald, GRADUATE, MA Hons (Geography) Durham.

Be himself so good, the Lord Mycroft, as a fellow varsity man to read and note my warnings – herein disclosed forthwith – in hopes that my deplorable unluckiness be relieved by more than a fish supper and litre of cooking lager.

My student days having finished, and employment inexplicably being unavailable at any remotely respectable establishment, I had no choice but to return to my childhood home. Indignities multiplied, and your honourable geographical servant soon found himself sleeping in bathing huts and subsiding on Pease Pudding detritus.

Fortune smiled on me, at last, when Ma Gypsum's Academy for Wretched Youths advertised an opening for a downtrodden sod to school imbeciles and near cretins, prior to their departure for some arse-end of the empire, therein to give the natives a damn good leathering.

'Holmes!' I ejaculated. 'Is there any point to this rambling and offensive document?'

'Pray have patience, my dear Watson. Events will soon gather pace.'

Somewhat reassured, I recommenced my perusal:

> *My only comfort, from a lonely garret room overlooking the broad sweeping bay, was to watch the crimson moon kissing those constant waters. Many is the night I have beheld its cheeks – sometimes damson, sometimes ivory – sink into aquatic slumber, only for your tireless writer to join it in welcome oblivion.*
>
> *Of late, however, my dreams have been disturbed by unaccountable horrors. Nightly it is that I am awakened by trumpet blasts, then the sight of those once delicate cheeks hovering over my gasping face, as I struggle for breath. It is as if the very moon itself has returned from Neptune's deeps, to scream and breathe foulness into the depths of my soul.*
>
> *So shaken am I by these events, I have had no choice but to quit the Gypsum household and seek temporary sanctuary, at a newly built Premier Inn, in Weymouth's disreputable outskirts.*
>
> *Alas, my lunar nemesis has now followed me even here! Amused locals have jeeringly informed that I am being hunted down by none other than Squatting Thomas, the much-feared progenitor of Spring-heeled Jack. This fiend preys on alumni of lesser universities, particularly those who dabble in execrable late-Romantic outpourings having reached the dizzying eminence of a degree in Geography.*
>
> *I beg you to forward this epistolary plea to your distinguished relative, a Mr Sherlock Holmes.*
>
> *I am forever in your debt and write as a gentleman.*
>
> *CORNELIUS GRISWALD MA (GEOGRAPHY, DURHAM).*

'The outpourings of a confirmed – probably syphilitic – lunatic?' I drily observed.

'Possibly, but I am minded to take the unfortunate Griswald's case – if for no other reason than to swap our London confinement for anywhere that can better distract my stagnant mind, however briefly.'

Holmes' much punctured inner left arm provided me with the only justification needed, for sending a swift telegram to the Premier Inn, informing our Durham man that his pleas had been heard.

The following morning found us gazing out at the wild but beautiful English Channel, its waves crashing over Weymouth's delicate Esplanade.

England's watering holes hold a certain grim majesty during the winter months, but it saddened me to see how far this Georgian beauty had declined into a late Victorian maelstrom of slapdash boarding houses, encrusted fried fish outlets and teetering scholastic establishments 'providing individual tuition by university men of known repute.'

Foremost in terms of decay was the fearsome sounding Gypsum Academy, to which Holmes – with his nose for direction and dereliction – led us in haste.

It would be difficult to imagine a more disgraceful establishment: the truly desperate would surely hesitate, before entrusting any offspring there. The redoubtable sounding 'Ma' was clearly combining pedagogic services with a thriving kebab outlet. Even at that early hour, a crowd of disreputable types could be seen, besmirching the morning air with fearsome eructations, littering the once proud pavements with their foetid detritus.

As an old India hand, I am horribly familiar with the street food eaten by our lower orders, yet even my constitution could not have stomached Ma's offerings. As if in some grotesque parody of higher education, the various comestibles were named after the constituent colleges of Griswald's ridiculous alma mater.

My attention was soon drawn to a jauntily dressed young man. His boater and blazer could not have provided a more incongruous sight, set amidst the drab greys and browns of that loutish assembly.

'I believe we have found Mr Cornelius Griswald, MA (Durham),' chortled Holmes.

Griswald bounded towards us, proffering his 'Castle College' kebab, eager as a young puppy with a rubber ball.

'Any news on your nocturnal hauntings, Griswald?' queried Holmes.

'Alas, this very night I was visited by Squatting Thomas!' wailed the unfortunate wretch.

'Let us dispose of that disgusting kebab, then you can provide all the details. Omit nothing, however seemingly trivial,' commanded my friend, reciting his time-honoured mantra.

We then found refuge in a lugubrious seaside cafe, catering to sundry mutton-chop whiskered revenants from the night-time economy. To my surprise, Holmes ordered full English breakfasts for the three of us, having thrown Griswald's vile snack seawards.

'Mr Holmes, I intend to speak frankly. Having reached the very pinnacle of scholastic achievement, my current predicament is proving intolerable!'

'Indeed?' drawled Holmes.

'My sole respite is the poetry of Algernon Charles Swinburne, consumed in prodigious quantities, whilst gazing over the boundless ocean lapping this small fragment of an all too sordid terra firma.'

To my amazement, Holmes suddenly delivered a ferocious steam hammering, pummelling Griswald's puny frame. Signalling me to join him, we drop-kicked the shit from this insufferable arse, with all his grotesque affectations and half-digested poesy.

In joyous scenes, which I now find difficult to recount without slipping into maudlin emotionalism, I saw my friend cast off his deplorable addiction, to revel in the innocent pleasure – the stout yeomanry – of pure English yobbery.

The entire establishment, realising things had 'kicked off', enthusiastically joined us in beating this snivelling pseud into oblivion.

In a coup de grace worthy of the London stage, two aging homosexualists hoisted Griswald onto the Formica counter, then spit roasted our gibbering geographer; an outrage fit to shock even Mr. Oscar Wilde and his entourage of Piccadilly decadents.

The doors finally swung open, revealing Griswald's nemesis.

Buttocks parted, Squatting Thomas – fresh from consuming several donners with chilli sauce at Ma Gypsum's – performed his unspeakable rights, over the semi-conscious Durham graduate.

I now understood the lunar references, as those shining moon cheeks opened and a sound – akin to a sail ripping on a four-mast tea clipper – rent the reeking air.

TripAdvisor provides a succinct yet reliable review of the Weymouth Premier Inn, where we later escorted the unfortunate Griswald. A power shower and several mugs of hotel hot chocolate all that were required, for his return to the rudest of health.

He now teaches Geography at a secondary school in Sutton-on-Sea, Lincolnshire – cured forever of his disastrous poetic habits.

TITLES BY PAUL SUTTON

Broadsheet Asphyxia (Original Plus, 2003).

The Chronicles of Dave Turnip (Original Plus, pamphlet, 2009).

Brains Scream at Night (BlazeVOX books, 2010).

Voiceover (with Rupert Loydell, The Knives, Forks and Spoons Press, pamphlet, 2011).

Indigo not Violet (The Red Ceilings Press, e-book, 2011).

Gemstones (The Red Ceilings Press, pamphlet, 2011).

Cabin Fever (The Knives, Forks and Spoons Press, 2012).

The Turnip's Return (The Red Ceilings Press, e-book, 2013).

Encouraging Signs (Shearsman, essays and interviews by Rupert Loydell; detailed interview on Sutton's poetry and poetics, 2013).

Falling Off (The Knives, Forks and Spoons Press, 2015 – Poetry Book Society Recommended Reading, Autumn 2015).

Taxi Drivers (The Red Ceilings Press, pamphlet, 2016).

To Say (Smallminded Books, pamphlet, 2016).

The Diversification of Dave Turnip (The Knives, Forks and Spoons Press, 2017).

The Sorry History of Fast Food (Leafe Press, pamphlet, 2017).

Parables for the Pouring Rain (BlazeVOX books, 2018).

Jack the Stripper (The Knives, Forks and Spoons Press, 2021 – Poetry Book Society Recommended Reading, Spring 2021).

Presents from my Boyfriends (The Red Ceilings Press, e-book, 2023).

9 781912 211982